SLEEP DISORDERS

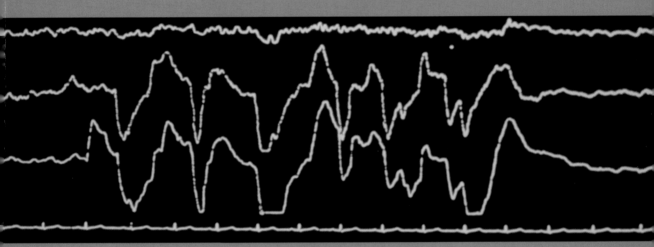

L. H. Colligan

Marshall Cavendish
Benchmark
New York

To people with sleep disorders everywhere

With thanks to Dr. Laurel Wills in the department of pediatrics at the Hennepin County Medical Center in Minneapolis, Minnesota, for her expert review of the manuscript.

Marshall Cavendish Benchmark
99 White Plains Road
Tarrytown, New York 10591-5502
www.marshallcavendish.us

Library of Congress Cataloging-in-Publication Data

Colligan, L. H.
Sleep disorders / by L.H. Colligan.
p. cm. — (Health alert)
Summary: "Provides comprehensive information on the causes, treatment, and history of sleep disorders"—Provided by publisher.
Includes index.
ISBN 978-0-7614-2913-5
1. Sleep disorders—Juvenile literature. I. Title.
RC547.C66 2009
616.8'498—dc22

2007034044

Front cover: The brain, highlighting the pineal gland, which secretes the hormone melatonin, which controls the body's biological clock
Title page: Brain patterns showing REM sleep

Photo Research by Candlepants Incorporated
Cover Photo: Alfred Pasieka / Photo Researchers Inc
The photographs in this book are used by permission and through the courtesy of:
Corbis: Tom & Dee Ann McCarthy, 5; Ed Young, 49. *PhotoTakeUSA.com*: BSIP, 7; Carol and Mike Werner, 24. *Getty Images*: Naile Goelbasi, 11; John Lamb, 15; Piotr Naskrecki, 20; Patti McConville, 26; Jaimie Travis, 44; Andy Cox, 47. *Photo Researchers Inc.*: Doug Martin, 12; James Holmes, 1, 19(Top & Lower); Chris Gallagher, 51; Garo, 54. *Sciencefaction.net*: Louie Psihoyos, 17, 38. *Super Stock*: Stock Image, 22. *AP Images*: AP Photo/Tribune-Review, Barry Reeger, 28. *Art Resource, NY*: Bildarchiv Preussischer Kulturbesitz, 36. *Alamy Images*: Mediacolor's, 30; Robin Nelson, 39; The Print Collector, 41; Sally and Richard Greenhill, 43; Photo Network, 46; ImageState, 33.

Editor: Joy Bean
Publisher: Michelle Bisson
Art Director: Anahid Hamparian

Printed in Malaysia
6 5 4 3 2 1

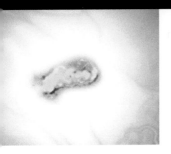

CONTENTS

WHAT IS IT LIKE TO HAVE A SLEEP DISORDER?

Maggie had been going to summer camp every year since she was eight. She and the other campers swam in the lake. They played team sports. They hiked the nearby trails. After lunch, they took naps, which Maggie had always enjoyed.

Things changed, though, when Maggie was twelve. Preteen campers no longer had to nap during quiet time. Instead, they could use the rest hour to read, write letters, or talk quietly. But Maggie still seemed to need her naps. The minute she lay on her bunk, she immediately fell into a deep sleep and had to have her bunkmates wake her up. She remembers that summer as the first time she realized she needed more sleep than other kids her age.

Maggie's sleep habits continued to be different from those of her friends throughout middle and high school. Sometimes she took several naps after school before she finally went to sleep for the night. Yet no matter how much she napped, she began to suffer what felt like sleep attacks during the day. They came over her so suddenly that she sometimes had to pinch her arm to stay awake in her classes.

Schoolwork became a struggle. Maggie often felt as if the information she read or tried to memorize did not stick in her brain. She could read a chapter of a book at night and not remember a thing about it the next morning. Before every test, she tried to memorize the material several times at night, then again in the early morning.

Staying awake and alert in school can be a constant struggle for a student who suffers from a sleep disorder.

When Maggie was a high school senior, her dad saw a news program about a sleeping disorder called **narcolepsy.** Just like Maggie, narcoleptics took frequent naps. Yet they were always tired. Many of them had a kind of fainting condition called **cataplexy.** Maggie had already had a couple scary episodes that happened when she was laughing hard about something with her friends. Suddenly her leg muscles had felt rubbery, and so had her face. Luckily, both times her friends had helped her to find a place to sit down. She later brushed off these spells as dizziness, but they had scared her.

Maggie's parents took her to a sleep disorder specialist. The doctor asked questions and listened carefully to the answers. The doctor examined Maggie and took blood samples to make sure Maggie did not have a medical condition that was not a sleep disorder. Finally, the doctor suggested that Maggie spend a night and a day at a sleep laboratory.

When Maggie arrived at the lab, a technician led her to a nice place that looked like a motel room. It had a comfortable bed, a night table, some lamps, and the machine the doctor had mentioned she would be using. The technician placed sensors over different places on Maggie's head and body and then turned off the lights. Maggie fell asleep immediately. The **polysomnograph** collected information all night long. After awakening the next morning, Maggie went for breakfast in the cafeteria. Afterward she returned to the lab to be monitored while she took a few naps.

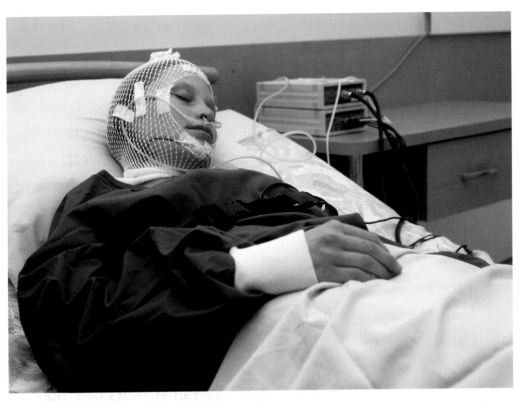

Machines in a sleep clinic, including polysomnographs, measure sleep patterns, breathing, heart rate, and leg movements in patients with sleep disorders.

A few days later, the sleep specialist met with Maggie and her parents again to discuss the test results. The doctor told Maggie she was lucky her dad had connected her symptoms to narcolepsy. That was Maggie's diagnosis. "Many narcoleptics do not get diagnosed for years," the doctor said. "More than 150,000 Americans have narcolepsy."

Maggie's sleep-wave patterns were typical of narcolepsy. The polysomnograph showed that Maggie got only short periods of **rapid eye movement (REM) sleep**. During this stage, a sleeper's eyes move rapidly, dreams are easier to recall, and the brain is as active as it is during the day. Maggie got REM sleep, but it came on too soon. The doctor pointed out that sleep interruptions like Maggie's cause memory problems. This was one of the reasons, besides tiredness, that Maggie had trouble remembering information for tests. Maggie's nap patterns were different too. She fell into REM sleep just one to two minutes after lying down for her naps. Most people without narcolepsy do not enter REM sleep during daytime naps at all.

Maggie felt both worried and relieved. She was unhappy about having a lifelong sleep problem. But she was relieved that her unusual sleep habits had a name. Now they could be treated. The doctor said Maggie could do most things teens her age did. She could play sports. She could drive. She could make plans for college. But to lead her normal life, Maggie would always need to take several naps a day. The doctor said she would contact Maggie's school so Maggie could be allowed to nap during free periods. She would also ask the school to allow Maggie to have extra study time before tests and extra test time. She gave Maggie a prescription for a medication that would eventually cut down on the number of sleep attacks Maggie experienced and help her to feel more alert.

Maggie still had to work extra hard at school. She got in the habit of writing down notes to herself so she would remember what she had to do. She took naps several times a day. With rest and medication, Maggie's cataplexy attacks became rare. She did well enough in high school to attend college. She still could not stay up for long hours the way her college friends did. Everyone understood that Maggie needed her sleep. It was no big deal. Maggie graduated from college with her friends. She later married and had a daughter who did not have narcolepsy. But Maggie did find out one interesting thing years later at a family reunion. A cousin and a great aunt had narcolepsy too. It ran in their family, just like Maggie's hazel eyes and blond hair.

2

WHAT ARE SLEEP DISORDERS?

Sleep disorders are conditions that cause sleeplessness, low quality sleep, and disturbed sleep and wakefulness cycles. In order to function well, nearly all birds and mammals, including humans, must regularly complete a sleep-wake cycle that lasts approximately twenty-four hours. This cycle seems to be as important for survival as oxygen, water, and food. Animal studies have shown that when researchers kept rats awake, the rats died prematurely, in two to three weeks. In a study of humans, people who slept fewer than six hours a night had a higher death rate than those who slept longer.

Sleep comes naturally to most people. Anyone might have a sleepless night once in a while. But most of the time, people fall asleep easily and remain asleep. This is not the case for people with sleep disorders. For them, falling asleep or staying asleep can be a nightly struggle. Others experience sleep disorders that trigger strange behaviors, such as **sleepwalking** or teeth grinding, that make them tired the next day.

People of all ages with sleep disorders face daily challenges. They are tired nearly all the time. Some sleepy students, including those with sleep disorders, fall asleep in class. Often their grades suffer because they are too tired to concentrate on their work. A 2007 study at Brown University compared the Monday morning school performance of two groups of teens. One group went to bed and got up at the same time every day. The second group stayed up late during the week,

Tired individuals miss out on the full benefits of healthy amounts sleep—cell repair that makes people feel rested the next day, growth hormone release, and protection from some illnesses.

then tried to catch up on sleep over the weekend. The weekend sleepers felt worse on Monday mornings and did worse in school than the students who went to bed and woke up at the same time every day.

Sleep disorders cause more problems than fatigue. Researchers have found that sleeplessness can cause some cases of obesity, heart disease, and a serious medical condition called diabetes. Diabetes occurs when the body stops making insulin, a substance the body needs to turn blood sugar into energy. In one study, people who averaged just five hours of sleep a night were more likely to gain weight than sleepers who slept several hours longer. In another study, young men were allowed to sleep only four hours a night for several nights. Afterward, their blood sugar levels increased to levels similar to those of prediabetics.

Sleep disorders also affect people's moods. Sleep-deprived people feel cranky. They can get impatient with family members, friends, teachers, coworkers, and bosses. Tired children have temper tantrums and "meltdowns" when they get frustrated—all because they are tired.

This sleeper's muscles are at rest, but other systems in the body are active during sleep.

Sleep disorders affect the public as well. Overtired drivers, including some people with untreated sleep disorders, cause approximately 100,000 traffic accidents, 1,500 deaths, and more than 70,000 injuries every year in the United States. Workers who are poorly rested make mistakes on the job that can cost money and affect safety. One 2003 study showed that doctors who had to work five shifts lasting twenty-four hours or more without sleep in a month made 700 percent more mistakes treating patients than doctors who got more sleep. What these studies show is that people cannot function well without regular periods of adequate sleep and wakefulness.

NORMAL SLEEP

Sleep disorders disrupt two important systems that influence the sleep-wake cycle. One system is called **homeostasis**. It keeps body temperature, blood pressure, and body chemistry in a balanced, healthy state. Homeostasis drives people to go to sleep when they feel tired.

Light and darkness are the strongest factors controlling the second system, called the **circadian rhythm**, or the biological clock. Light coming in through the eyes sets this clock and tells the body it is daytime, and thus time to be alert. When no light comes in at night, a part of the brain, the **pineal gland**, releases **melatonin.** This chemical makes people feel sleepy.

People feel most rested when their homeostasis and circadian rhythms are in sync. That is when normal, refreshing sleep can occur. For someone with a sleep disorder, those systems may be out of sync. For example, if a person takes a long nap during the day, he or she might not feel the homeostatic need for sleep at a usual or natural bedtime.

Normal sleep is a little like a computer in sleep mode. The computer may be receiving e-mails, running antivirus software, and performing other tasks even when the screen is dark. In a similar way, the brain performs important tasks while a sleeper's eyes are closed and some parts of the body are functioning in a slowed state. Just as a computer in sleep mode uses less energy, so does a human body that is sleeping.

Yet during the downtime of sleep, the brain performs many tasks to restore itself. Among other things, it uses some of the sleep time to repair, heal, and replace damaged cells that get worn out during waking hours.

Not only cell repair takes place during sleep. While a sleeper is at rest, the brain also directs the release of **hormones** throughout the body's major systems. These important substances affect growth, appetite, and sexual characteristics. Some of these hormones affect the digestive system during sleep. Studies have shown that people who do not get the sleep they need are more likely to become overweight than those who sleep well. Some researchers believe that reduced sleep time may cause an imbalance in a hormone called leptin, which tells

Teens and Sleep

Teenagers do not suddenly decide they have to go to bed later when they hit adolescence. Their body clocks, or circadian rhythms, are actually reset. Melatonin release takes place later at night in teens than it does in children and adults. Unfortunately, middle and high school schedules are run by school clocks, not biological clocks. Doing the math points out the problem teens have in getting the nine or ten hours of sleep they need. They need that much sleep because so much is going on at once. Their bodies and brains are growing fast. They are going through puberty, the period during which sexual characteristics develop. They are building up more fat and muscle. But school schedules make it hard for most teens in the United States to get all the zzz's they need. Adolescent brains do not signal sleepiness until about eleven o'clock or later at night. This becomes a problem because most teens need to get up at six or seven in the morning. The sleep numbers do not add up to a good night's sleep for today's teenagers.

Most fully rested people do not need an alarm clock to awaken.

Findings about the circadian rhythm shift and delayed melatonin release in adolescents came out in the 1990s. Educators began to discuss the possibility of moving high school start times later. The Minneapolis Public School District in Minnesota did just that. The district decided to see what would happen if some of their high schools started at 8:40 A.M. instead of 7:15 A.M. This gave students more than seven extra hours of sleep a week. Teachers reported that students' alertness improved. So did school attendance levels. And students reported lower levels of **depression**.

the body to get more calories from food the next day. Other hormones released during normal sleep affect the cardiovascular system, which pumps blood through the body. A 2003 study of women showed that those who slept fewer than five hours a night had more heart problems than women who averaged eight hours of sleep. Some researchers believe that a lack of sleep may have caused the subjects' bodies to release the stress hormone **cortisol**, which may increase the risk of heart attacks.

People who do not get enough sleep over long stretches of time are more likely than rested individuals to catch the flu and common colds. That is because during healthy sleep certain cells build up immunities, which fight off infections. One 2002 study showed that men who got only four hours of sleep a night for six nights created half the number of infection-fighting antibodies after getting flu shots than did sleepers who slept longer.

Researchers believe the brain performs other tasks while a person is sleeping normally. It seems to organize events, learning experiences, and feelings the sleeper had during the day. Some of this information is then stored as memories, which can be used later. A major 2006 animal study at the Massachusetts Institute of Technology (MIT) seems to support this idea. Researchers determined that during sleep, rats replayed memories of tasks they had learned during the day. Dr. Larry Squire, a scientist who studies memory, said of the

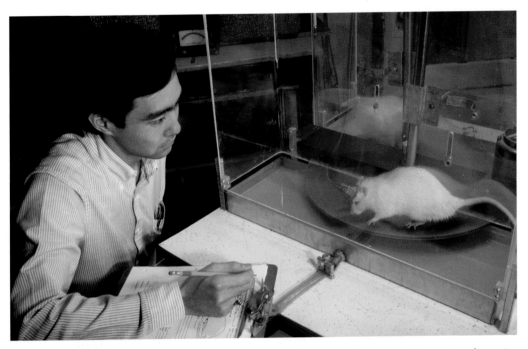

Animal studies on sleep-deprived rats have shown that they die sooner than rats who get normal amounts of sleep.

MIT study that the fact that these memory replays occurred during sleep "would certainly provide one clue that part of the function of sleep is to let us process and stabilize the experiences we have during the day."

All of the tasks that go on during normal sleep take time. The brain cannot fully complete all its important work when people do not get enough sleep. People who sleep late on the weekends may believe they can catch up on sleep, but their brains cannot. Poor sleepers develop a sleep debt that is hard to pay back.

How Much Sleep Do People Need?

....

A few extremely rare people called short sleepers can truly get by on four or five hours of sleep. But everyone else needs much more. Infants, children, and teenagers need the most sleep. They are growing more and learning more new information than adults. Their immune systems are immature. During long hours of normal sleep, the body builds up this system.

What is the right amount of sleep for each age? Sleep experts recommend that individuals sleep until they feel rested and energized for the way they live. Here are some general recommendations at different stages of life:

- Children 6–12: About 10 to 12 hours
- Teens 13–20: At least 9 to 10 hours
- Adults 25 and up: 7 to 8 hours, although elderly people may need a little less

Normal, healthy sleep takes place in cycles made up of five stages. Here is what usually happens during normal sleep in each of these cycles:

Stage 1
- The sleeper dozes off, is still dimly aware of sur- roundings—outside temper- ature, noise, and light—and then moves into light sleep. This stage usually lasts for less than ten minutes.

Stage 2
- Awareness of surroundings fades away.
- The sleeper's body tempera- ture drops.
- Breathing and heart rates slow down then hold steady.

Stages 3 and 4
- Slow-wave sleep continues.

- Blood pressure decreases.
- Heart and breathing rates continue to slow down.
- Cell repair takes place throughout the body and brain. These two sleep stages strongly contribute to a feeling of being rested upon awakening.
- Slow-wave sleep takes place, a process which, along with REM sleep, may aid in learning, as the brain processes events, experiences, and information from the day and stores some of them as memories.
- The brain directs various organs to release hormones related to growth, appetite, and sexual characteristics.

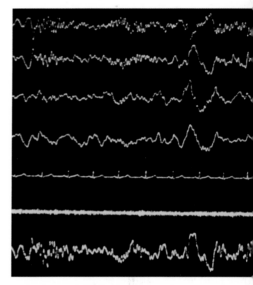

About 50 percent of total sleep time occurs during stage 2 sleep.

REM Sleep

- The eyes move rapidly back and forth, with the eyelids closed.
- Breathing and heart rates speed up.
- Blood pressure rises.
- Muscles totally relax and the body is still, except for some twitching.
- Dreaming takes place.

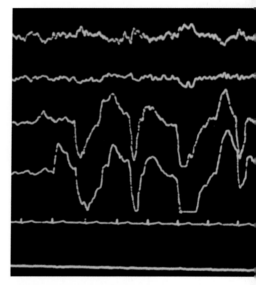

REM sleep helps the brain to restore energy spent during the day.

WHAT GOES WRONG

Sleep disorders can disrupt the sleep-wake cycle and the five stages of healthy sleep. A disorder may interrupt stages, shorten them, or keep them from taking place. A disorder may cause a sleeper to engage in unusual physical behaviors that tire out the sleeper the next day. As a result, someone with a sleep disorder does not get the full benefits that normal sleep brings.

COMMON SLEEP DISORDERS

More than eighty sleep disorders disturb the sleep of infants, children, teenagers, and adults around the world. However, only about a dozen of them cause the majority of sleep problems.

Fifty to seventy thousand people a year in Africa suffer a kind of sleeping sickness due to tsetse fly bites.

Some disorders seem to run in families, such as bed-wetting, sleepwalking, and narcolepsy. Alcohol use, drug use, and certain physical or mental illnesses cause other sleep problems. Jet lag, the schedules of people who work at night, and poor sleep habits can trigger circadian rhythm sleep disorders. The causes of some sleep disorders, such as teeth grinding, are not completely known.

The most common sleep disorders are generally grouped by their symptoms. The **dyssomnias** include sleep disorders that cause people to have trouble falling asleep or staying asleep.

People who suffer from **delayed sleep phase syndrome (DSPS)** experience a circadian rhythm disorder that makes it difficult for them to fall asleep until the middle of the night on most nights. As a result, they have great difficulty waking up on time if school or work starts too early for them. The disorder often develops when night owls get in the habit of going to bed late. Too many late nights reset their biological clocks.

Hypersomnia is defined as excessive sleepiness during one's waking hours. Hypersomniacs may need to sleep for twelve hours or more every day. Despite oversleeping, hypersomniacs remain groggy, confused, and disoriented. They are often over-weight due to inactivity. The condition is usually permanent, though it can be managed.

Insomnia sufferers have a hard time falling sleep and staying asleep. Sometimes they wake up too early to feel rested. Periods of insomnia can last just a few nights or for

Females are more likely than males to experience insomnia. Many researchers believe this occurs because female hormone levels fluctuate more than male hormone levels do.

long stretches that occur on and off throughout a person's life. It is the most common sleep disorder, and it can have many causes. About 12 percent of sleepers have insomnia at one time or another. According to a 2004 study, many teens in the United States have periodic insomnia. The problem usually starts around the age of eleven. Girls are most likely to get insomnia after they first get their menstrual period.

Poor sleep habits are the major cause of insomnia. This sleep disorder may develop in adults who repeatedly stay up too late. Insomnia can show up in infants, babies, and children if parents allow them to stay up even when they are tired. The body deals with overtiredness in several ways. It may release stimulating chemicals such as adrenaline to keep someone going. Most people have seen overtired, out-of-control children. Adrenaline overstimulates the tired child—or adult— with a temporary boost of energy and alertness. Without rest, levels of the stress hormone cortisol remain high. The result, particularly in children, is irritability, excitability, and difficulty falling asleep despite being exhausted. Normal sleep patterns are disrupted, and the conditions for insomnia are set.

Besides poor sleep habits, certain medical conditions, such as Parkinson's disease, asthma, arthritis, and pain, can cause insomnia. Elderly people may develop insomnia because of such physical problems, depression or, for example, a daytime habit of napping for too long. Anxiety, stress, worry, depression, and panic attacks contribute to insomnia. Stimulating caffeinated beverages, such as coffee, certain teas, and energy drinks, are known to interfere with sleep and lead to insomnia.

Narcolepsy is a disorder in an area of the brain that affects sleep. The narcoleptic brain cannot regulate the sleep-wake cycle. Narcoleptics seem to lack a brain chemical called hypocretin, which is related to alertness. Narcolepsy is more common than once thought. It sometimes runs in families. It affects about one in two thousand people in the United States. Most narcoleptics develop the disorder in their teen years or in their twenties.

The symptoms of narcolepsy include multiple daily spells of extreme sleepiness that can strike at almost any time. When narcoleptics do sleep, their non-REM and REM sleep stages are abnormal. Narcoleptics may also experience bouts of **sleep paralysis**. Temporary loss of muscle control is a normal part of REM sleep that prevents sleepers from physically acting out their dreams. However, narcoleptics experience sleep paralysis while they are awake and aware. Sleep paralysis is different from the muscle weakness that causes cataplexy. The majority of narcoleptics get attacks of cataplexy, which may cause them to fall and injure themselves because of their weakened muscles.

Restless leg syndrome (RLS) causes the urge to perform foot or leg movements. Sufferers experience a tingling or burning sensation in their feet or legs that gets worse when they lie down. They get some relief from moving their legs. Some possible causes include family history, drinking too much caffeine, pregnancy, low iron levels in the blood, and certain diseases such as arthritis, kidney failure, and rheumatoid arthritis. Interrupted sleep can cause those who have RLS to feel next-day grogginess, lack of concentration, and fatigue.

Restless leg syndrome interferes with healthy stages of sleep.

Sleep apnea is a common disorder that causes people to pause in their breathing during sleep for ten seconds or more. Almost 18 million Americans have this disorder. It can be mild or severe. The number of sufferers is increasing because obesity is increasing. Being overweight is one major cause of obstructive sleep apnea (OSA). Fatty neck tissue interferes with the workings of the soft tissue at the back of the throat and the windpipe. When these areas get squeezed, the soft tissue collapses. This temporarily blocks airflow from the nose and mouth to the lungs. Weak muscle tone in elderly people can also cause the soft tissue collapse that leads to apnea. For children, snoring and sleep apnea are usually caused by enlarged adenoids or tonsils.

In central sleep apnea (CSA), breathing is interrupted due to an abnormality in the part of the brain that controls breathing. To "save" the sleeper, the brain usually wakes up the person to restart normal breathing.

As a result of interrupted breathing, sufferers of both types of sleep apnea are constantly tired. They find it hard to concentrate, to remember information, and to stay alert. Adults with OSA can therefore develop high blood pressure and irregular heartbeats. They are at high risk for strokes and heart attacks. People with sleep apnea are sometimes involved in car accidents due to excessive fatigue, slow reaction time, and the inability to concentrate after constant nights of interrupted

Snoring

If someone started a vacuum cleaner in the middle of the night, it would produce a sound as loud as some sleepers' snoring. Some sleepers snore when they inhale air through the mouth. If the narrow passages in the nose or throat touch each other, they vibrate as air passes through. The result is the snoring sound. Most snoring just annoys nearby sleepers. The causes of temporary snoring may be having allergies, a cold, a throat infection, or a structural nose blockage, taking certain medications, or drinking alcohol. However, frequent, loud snoring in children and adults can be a symptom of sleep apnea. Apnea snoring can sound as loud as a leaf blower. The sleeper produces gasping sounds as he or she struggles to breathe after breathing has stopped. Snoring due to apnea can go on all night long because sleep apnea causes many breathing interruptions.

Snoring often affects the sleep quality of both the snoring sleeper and those trying to sleep nearby.

sleep. Sleep apnea can be treated so that people with this condition can feel alert, well rested, and energetic and lead healthy lives.

Parasomnia is a second category of sleep disorders that includes involuntary behaviors that interfere with sleep such, as sleeptalking and sleepwalking. Most childhood sleep disorders are parasomnias. They usually take place when there is a disruption in sleep stages.

Bed-wetting, also known as **nocturnal enuresis**, mainly affects children. Some of them never had control of urination due to urinary tract infections or hormonal problems. Other bed wetters sleep so deeply that they do not feel the urge to use the bathroom during sleep. Millions of children wet their beds occasionally or sometimes regularly. The vast majority of children outgrow bed-wetting as their bodies and brains mature. Many bed wetters have family members who were also bed wetters as children.

Bruxism, or teeth grinding, can begin in infancy, as soon as the teeth come in. The habit may go on into childhood. Some adults start to grind their teeth later in life. Not all causes of the disorder are known, though anxiety in adults is sometimes associated with bruxism. So is taking certain antidepressants. Teeth grinding may harm the teeth and gum tissue. In these cases, people can wear a mouth guard to maintain their dental health.

Infant and child sleep apnea is a condition that causes a child to stop breathing many times during sleep. It can be a life-threatening disorder because it robs the body of the oxygen it needs to stay alive. The causes of apnea in children may include premature birth, allergies, frequent colds, daytime breathing difficulties, enlarged tonsils or adenoids in the throat and nose area, or obesity that causes a buildup of fatty tissue in the neck area. Usually, the affected infants or children awaken in time to begin breathing again. They may not remember these interruptions the next day. However, they will be very tired from repeated awakenings. Symptoms of sleep apnea include snoring, irregular breathing, mouth breathing during sleep, excessive tiredness during the day, bedwetting, frequent nightmares, irritability, learning difficulties, frequent respiratory infections, hyperactivity, headaches, as well as other symptoms.

A breathing machine may be needed to help children and adults who have sleep apnea.

Rhythmic movement disorder (RMD) includes nighttime head banging and body rocking in children, usually under the age of four. The movement may begin as a calming activity to help the child fall asleep. However, it continues after the child does fall asleep. The child does not control the banging and rocking or remember it the next day. In some rare cases, a child may have a neurological problem in the brain that causes the banging. Children usually outgrow the disorder.

Sleep terrors are a type of disorder that causes a child to begin screaming, crying, and thrashing during deep, slow-wave, non-REM sleep. These children usually have no memory of being upset. Approximately 5 percent of children have sleep terrors between the ages of four and twelve. Sleep terrors are not the same as nightmares, which take place during REM sleep. During sleep terror, the child may resist being comforted. More boys than girls suffer sleep terrors. These disturbances usually end during adolescence.

Sleepwalking causes a sleeper—usually a child or preteen—to get out of bed while still in a state of non-REM, slow-wave sleep. He or she may walk around with eyes open, sometimes crying, sometimes picking up real or imagined objects. Younger children are much more likely than adolescents or adults to walk in their sleep. It is thought that this is because children experience long periods of slow-wave sleep, when most sleep-walking takes place. Some sleepwalkers get dressed, go to the

Sleepwalkers do not usually recall their sleepwalking the next day because they were sound asleep.

kitchen for food, or open and close doors. Studies have shown that identical twins tend to share this behavior. Therefore, family history probably plays a role in the development of some sleepwalking. More incidents may occur when a sleeper is stressed out, overly tired, or sick, but most happen in perfectly healthy kids.

Sudden infant death syndrome (SIDS) causes the deaths of at least 4,500 babies a year in the United States. The babies, who die while sleeping, are usually between the ages of one month and one year old. The death rate today is lower than it was before 1990. That is when doctors began to educate parents about possible causes of SIDS. These risks include premature birth, low birth weight, babies sleeping on their stomachs, putting loose blankets and sheets around the baby, overheating, smoking in the household, bed sharing, or a previous SIDS death of another baby in the family. However, no single cause has been found yet. A report in 2006 stated that some babies who died of SIDS had abnormalities in parts of the brain involved in the control of breathing. A 2007 study showed an association between SIDS and damage to the newborn's inner right ear during birth.

New technologies are making it possible for brain and sleep researchers to discover more causes of sleep disorders such as SIDS, sleep apnea, and insomnia. Understanding these causes will lead to more treatments for sleeping disorders that have been around as long as humans.

3

THE HISTORY OF SLEEP DISORDERS

It is the middle of the night in a place far away from cities and towns. The small hut is crowded. Several people are moving around or sitting by the fire that lights the space. Most of the sleepers will move in and out of wakefulness all night long. They are lying on straw mats or directly on the ground. None of the sleepers have pillows. The babies sleep close to their mothers. Several people snore loudly. Just outside, the group's animals are making loud sounds as well. It is hard to believe anyone can sleep with the racket going on in this crowded sleep space.

What a contrast to sleeping quarters in the modern Western world. Many people sleep by themselves or with one other person in darkened, silent bedrooms warmed by heat or cooled by air-conditioning. They rest their bodies under blankets and lie on thick mattresses and puffy pillows. Their children often have their own rooms. If people cannot sleep despite all these

Comfortable mattresses, pillows, quilts, room-darkening shades, and sleeping pills have become billion-dollar industries as people seek ways to get a good night's sleep.

comforts, some of them begin to wonder whether they have sleeping disorders.

Anthropologists, the scientists who study new and old cultures, have begun to study the sleeping habits of non-Western people in remote parts of Africa, Australia, Indonesia, Pakistan, and South America. People there follow sleeping patterns that were common in the West until about two hundred years ago. That is when factory work—industrialization—began. The old ways of sleeping changed. People began to work and sleep by the clock. They needed to have specific bedtimes because they had specific times to start work. Sleeping straight through the night became important. One anthropologist, Carol Worthman of Emory University in Atlanta, Georgia, thinks older ways of sleeping have something to teach modern sleepers. "It's time for scientists to get out into natural sleep environments," Worthman advises. She has discovered that sleepers in traditional cultures have long stretches of rest time after dark but no specific bedtimes or wake-up times. They share sleep spaces. Sleeping in groups provides safety and the warmth of body heat. Group members sleep on mats, platforms, or the ground. Not requiring beds means sleepers can sleep almost anywhere. Babies are used to sleeping with noise and movement, and they doze whenever they are tired. Adults sometimes stay up all night to perform rituals. This teaches the group how to get by on very little sleep if it needs to. On most nights, group members sleep in two separate blocks of time. They can check on the fire, watch the animals, and look out for danger before sleeping again. Traditional groups usually go to sleep wearing the clothes they wear during the day. They are dressed for escape if they need to get away quickly. Sleeping off and on is safer than sleeping straight through the night, which is the modern standard.

One modern sleep study mimicked this natural environment. Psychiatrist Thomas A. Wehr of the National Institute of Mental Health designed an experiment with fifteen adults. They were to sleep or rest during a fourteen-hour darkened period, from six in the evening until eight in the morning, over several weeks. At first the volunteers slept straight through for about eleven hours to catch up on sleep. After that, their sleep patterns shifted. They lay awake quietly for a couple hours or so in the early evening. Then they slept anywhere from three to five hours, followed by wakefulness for an hour or so. Finally, they slept in a second block of about four hours until it was light in the morning. This experiment shows that, given the chance, modern humans are inclined to sleep in the traditional way. Unfortunately, the demands of modern work and school schedules make it difficult to devote eleven to fourteen hours to rest and sleep. The result may be sleep disorders.

Sleep problems are more than two hundred years old. One of the first references to sleep problems appears in an ancient Egyptian text that says one of the worst things in life is "to be in bed and sleep not." Busy Egyptians, who lived in settlements and not as hunter-gatherers, valued sleep and the dreams that came with it. An ancient papyrus recommends an overnight treatment at a sleep temple and also mentions "a woman who loves bed, she does not rise, and does not shake it."

In 400 BCE, the Greek doctor Hippocrates offered advice for healthy sleep. He warned about the emotional and physical problems that result from a lack of sleep:

With regard to sleep—as is usual with us in health,
the patient should wake during the day and sleep during

the night. If this rule by anywise altered it is so far worse . . . but the worst of all is to get no sleep either night or day; for it follow from this symptom that the insomnolency [sleeplessness] is connected with sorrow and pains, or that he is about to become delirious.

The ancient Romans had their own god of sleep, Somnus, from whom the word insomnia came. The Latin word means sleepless. Like the Greeks and probably the Egyptians before them, the Romans used opium as a sleep medication in addition to valerian root and the chamomile plant. These plants are still

Even Greek gods needed to sleep.

used today as natural sleep medications. In the Middle Ages, one sleep aid included sponges soaked with wine and herbs.

In the 1800s, the previously held notion that blood traveled out of the brain during sleep changed. Doctors began to believe that the brain, not the heart and blood vessels, controlled sleep. Between the 1800s and 1900s, scientists developed other theories about sleep. Some thought that a sleeping body was in a kind of drunken state, a coma, or an animal-like hibernation. Others believed loss of oxygen caused people to fall asleep. Some suggested that poisonous toxins accumulated in the body during the day and then drained away during sleep. Without a complete understanding of specific sleep problems, many sleepless people continued to treat themselves with the same strong medications—opium and alcohol. It is now known that alcohol is a major disrupter of sleep. Morphine, made from opium, is now used mainly as a painkiller and must be prescribed by a doctor.

Sleep theories changed again when some scientists began to observe the natural rhythms of plants, animals, and insects in the early 1900s. They saw the effects of light and darkness on flowers, bees, and rats. They noted that human body temperature changes during the day and at night. Scientists developed the first notions about the circadian rhythm in people. However, many still viewed sleep as an inactive time with little or no brain activity.

The development of the electroencephalograph (EEG) machine

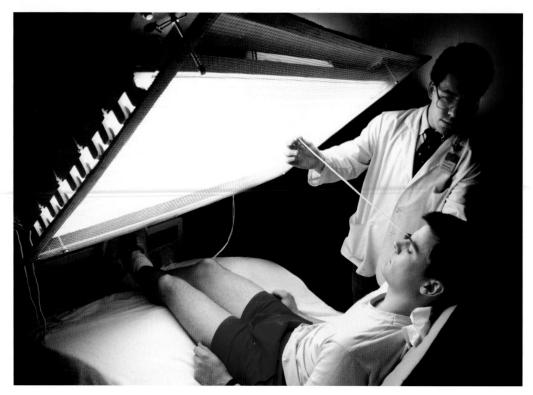
Light therapy can help those who have problems falling asleep and staying asleep.

in 1929 made it possible to measure electrical activity in the brain during sleep. In 1937, the EEG led to the classification of the five sleep stages. The EEG led to a greater understanding of the science of sleep and its disorders as well as the discovery of REM sleep in the 1950s.

More recent technology for studying sleep includes the magnetoencephalograph (MEG). This machine enables sleep researchers to study brain activity during sleep on a more sophisticated level. This new technology may be able to pinpoint the location in the brain of dreams that play back information from the subjects' daytime learning. Polysomnography provides an overall measurement of brain, heart, muscle, and lung activity during sleep. The multiple sleep latency test (MSLT) records sleep patterns.

During the middle of the twentieth century, more information about sleep disorders led to new treatments and medications for abnormal sleep. Doctors began to prescribe stimulants such as amphetamines for narcoleptics and hypersomniacs. New technologies that could monitor breathing helped researchers

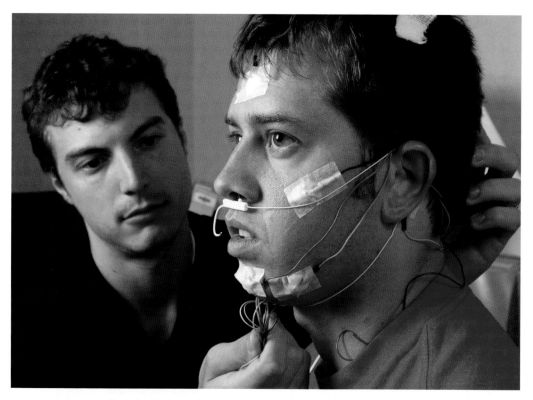

The invention of the electroencephalograph (EEG) helped scientists realize that the brain is active during sleep and that sleep disorders disrupt this activity.

learn more about the role of breathlessness in sleep apnea. The continuous positive airway pressure (CPAP) machine, invented in the 1980s, became a standard treatment for stabilizing breathing in sleep apnea patients. The machine blows cool air into the mouth of a sleeper who is wearing a mask attached to the CPAP machine. This keeps the airways open.

By 1969, relaxation techniques and hypnosis came into use as treatments for insomnia. The Egyptians had used these methods thousands of years before! In the 1980s, scientists developed other nondrug therapies including **biofeedback** machines and cognitive behavioral therapy (CBT). These behavioral techniques taught troubled sleepers how and when to relax themselves to get to sleep and to stay asleep. Today, some experts recommend sleep restriction and stimulus control to help people with sleep disorders manage their wakefulness so they can sleep better at night.

Today, it is hard to turn on the television or read a magazine without seeing commercials for sleeping pills. The newest medications are part of a long line of sleep-inducing drugs that evolved from opium use in ancient times. For centuries after that, many people with sleep problems continued to use plant-based sleep aids, including alcohol.

In the 1800s, a powerful sleeping medication called chloral hydrate put people to sleep quickly, especially when it was combined with alcohol. However, the combination of these two depressants was dangerous and habit-forming. Other man-made chemical sleep aids followed.

Today's sleeping drugs, the benzodiazepines, have largely replaced a class of habit-forming, man-made drugs called barbiturates, which were widely available sleeping pills in the first half of the twentieth century. Benzodiazepines are less likely than barbiturates to cause dependence.

In 1832, a German chemist, Justus von Liebig, created a chemical compound called chloral hydrate to help people fall asleep.

Improving the diagnosis of sleep disorders and managing them with lifestyle changes have transformed their treatment. More than one thousand licensed sleep disorder centers in the United States offer a full menu of treatments—including hypnosis and biofeedback—for the scores of sleep disorders that keep people awake. If tired, sleep-deprived ancient people came back today, they would have far more choices for solving their sleep problems than visiting a sleep temple to get a good night's sleep.

4

LIVING WITH A SLEEP DISORDER

Many people live with sleep disorders but do not have to. Sleep education and **sleep hygiene**—the practice of good sleep habits—can prevent certain common sleep disorders as well as treat some of them. These treatments can often be done at home. Generally, however, the most serious sleep disorders—narcolepsy, hypersomnia, sleep apnea, and sudden infant death syndrome—do require medical attention.

IS IT A SLEEP DISORDER?

The first step in treating a sleep problem is to find out whether the sleep-deprived person actually has a disorder. Both self-treatment and medical treatment begin when the patient answers questions about his or her sleep symptoms and habits. These are the most common questions asked to determine the existence of a disorder:

Some experts tell insomnia sufferers to avoid looking at clocks or watches in order to prevent anxiety that may increase sleeplessness.

- Does it regularly take you a long time to fall asleep at night?
- Do you frequently wake up during the night and have trouble going back to sleep?
- Do you wake up earlier than you want to? Or do you have trouble getting up for school or work in the morning?
- Do you wake up feeling out of breath during the night?
- Do you frequently have nightmares that wake you up?
- Do you snore heavily when you are asleep? (You might not know this yourself. Ask someone in your family if you snore.)
- Do you grind your teeth while asleep?
- Do you walk in your sleep?
- Are you tired on most days? Do you fall asleep at school or work?

Regular sleep habits at bedtime can reduce daytime sleepiness.

- Have you tried to follow good sleep habits—sleep hygiene—for several weeks, yet still cannot sleep?
- Do you have health problems—depression, asthma, allergies, or other sicknesses—that might be interfering with sleep?

Anyone who answers yes to half these questions should talk to a trusted adult about home treatments to see if they cure the sleeping problem. Possible medical treatment may be needed if self-treatment does not fix the problem.

Most people who sleep normally do not need a perfectly comfortable room, at the perfect temperature, with total silence or darkness. Healthy daytime activities, a little exercise, and going to bed at the right time are often enough to help most people get a good night's sleep.

BEHAVIOR CHANGES AND SLEEP

Many sleepers take their worries to bed. Sometimes they push away their worries during the day, only to have them reappear in the middle of the night. Several techniques can help anxious sleepers relax. One, called guided imagery, changes thoughts from worries to relaxing ones. Here is one way to do it. While lying in bed, take several deep breaths in a slow rhythm. Slowly close your eyes. Envision your worries as specks on a windshield. Slowly picture gentle rain and the windshield wipers washing away those specks until the glass is clear. Now picture a beautiful or enjoyable scene from your past just beyond the windshield. Keep breathing regularly. Imagine yourself driving into that scene and away from the troubles of the day.

Muscle relaxation is another way many people learn to bring on sleep. Lie back in bed. Beginning with your hands, clench your fists and then relax them completely. Do this several times. Work your way up your arm, shoulder, and neck muscles, tensing them, then very slowly relaxing them. Do the same with your feet, legs, hips, and stomach muscles. Finally, scrunch your face muscles, then slowly relax them. If you are still awake, begin the windshield wiper imagery exercise to create pleasant images for falling asleep.

Deep-breathing exercises can be relaxing for many kids and adults. To try these exercises, lie down on your bed.

Sleep Hygiene and You

These healthy sleep habits can often prevent sleep disorders from developing or cure some that already exist:

- Try to exercise every day, but not too close to bedtime. Exercise relieves the stress and worries that often keep people awake.
- Maintain a healthy weight through exercise and eating nutritious food. Being overweight is a major risk factor for sleep apnea in both adults and children.
- Eat the last meal of the day a few hours before bedtime, at about the same time every evening. This way, your body does not have to work overtime by digesting food while it is putting you to sleep.

Children and adults who exercise regularly experience more frequent deep-sleep stages that help them feel rested the next day.

- Avoid caffeinated drinks, such as colas, energy drinks, or coffee, especially in the afternoon or evening. Cut down on all liquids a few hours before going to bed.
- Have a regular bedtime that works with your family's wake-up time for school or work. Go to sleep and wake up at about the same time every day, including weekends.
- If you cannot fall asleep, keep the lights dim and read or do a quiet activity until you feel drowsy.
- Send dogs and cats to sleep in other rooms to see if you sleep better without them.
- Make light and darkness work for you. At night, begin to dim the lights about an hour before bedtime. Fading light sends a signal to your brain to release melatonin, which promotes sleep. If you cannot sleep without a light, keep a night-light on outside your room. If possible, ask someone to come in and open your shades after you fall asleep or before you wake up. The early-morning light will help your brain wake you up.

Soft light and quiet activities such as reading can help people get ready for a good night's sleep.

- Follow a nightly routine to prepare your body and brain for sleep. Wash up or take a shower or bath, put on pajamas, and brush your teeth. Use the bathroom so you do not have to get up later. Say good night to the phone, computer, television, and music.

Gently place your hands on your stomach. Breathe deeply through your nose. Feel your abdomen rise as your lungs fill with air. Hold each breath a little longer than you normally would. Release your breath through your mouth slowly. Listen to your breath leaving your lungs. Follow up with the windshield wiper imagery, and allow a pleasant remembered scene to fill your mind.

When at-home methods—sleep hygiene, imagery, and relaxation techniques—still do not work, professional guidance can help. In cognitive behavioral therapy (CBT), a therapist helps a sleepless person identify negative behaviors, such as saying, "I hate my bed. I can never fall asleep." Replacing such negative thoughts with positive ones comes next. "I do not have to fall asleep right away. I can always get up for a while, then go back to bed when I am sleepier." This way of thinking sets the stage for developing positive sleep habits. Short-term CBT has been very successful in having long-term positive effects, because kids and adults learn new skills they can use in the future.

MEDICAL TREATMENTS

Developing positive sleep behaviors is a starting place for treating all sleep disorders. However, narcolepsy, hypersomnia, sleep apnea in adults and babies, and insomnia associated with conditions such as depression or pain usually require medical attention. In such cases, the person with a sleep disorder must work out a sleep plan with a doctor. Treatments may require a visit to a sleep lab, medication, or the use of sleep aids, such as a breathing machine for sleep apnea or a light box to reset an abnormal circadian rhythm.

PREVENTING AND TREATING COMMON SLEEP DISORDERS

Bed-wetting is usually a temporary condition that almost all healthy children outgrow. Patience, not shame, is the best treatment. Parents

Sleep lab tests help doctors diagnose and treat serious sleep disorders.

of a child who has never been dry at night can try several preventive tactics to manage bed-wetting. The child should have a regularly scheduled dinnertime and a calm bedtime routine every evening. Fluids should be completely stopped after dinner. Any caffeine should be completely avoided, since it stimulates urination. The child should use the bathroom right before going to bed. Leave a light on near the bathroom so the child is not afraid to get up in the dark. Many disposable products are available to make cleanup easier until the child outgrows the disorder. If bed-wetting develops after a child has been toilet trained, then the child should see a doctor about this problem. A urinary tract infection or other medical condition may be causing the bedwetting.

Bruxism—teeth grinding—is more common in children than in adults. Calm, regular bedtime routines with dim lights can help a child—or an adult—relax before falling asleep. If teeth grinding starts to wear down the teeth, a dentist can provide a bite plate for the patient to wear to bed.

Delayed phase sleep syndrome (DPSP) sufferers are the night owls who reset their biological clocks with too many late nights. They may need a sleep specialist to help them reset their circadian rhythms. One effective treatment is light therapy using a light box that mimics sunlight. The patient sits in front of the prescribed light box in the morning. At night, the patient dims the lights, then turns them off entirely a little earlier each night. Another treatment calls for patients to go to sleep at ever-later times over a week or so. For example, if patients usually go to bed at 1:00 A.M. they push their bedtime ahead to 3:00 A.M. The next night, they push the sleeping time forward by another few hours. By pushing forward their bedtimes over many nights, the DPSP sleepers will eventually arrive at a more normal bedtime of 10:00 P.M. or so and will have an easier time awakening.

Hypersomniacs, those who require much more sleep than average, usually begin treatment for their disorder by getting a physical exam. Their inactivity may be associated with obesity or simply a lack of physical fitness because they are too tired to exercise. These problems must be treated along with the sleep disorder. The doctor may recommend that the patient see a sleep specialist. Hypersomnia is usually not curable. However, it can be managed with medication. The sleep specialist may prescribe stimulants to keep the patient awake and alert during the day.

Infant and childhood sleep apnea has several causes, so treatments vary. Some doctors remove the child's tonsils or adenoids to open up the airways. A doctor may advise an obese child to slim down so that fatty tissues in the neck do not block breathing. A doctor may recommend a continuous positive airway pressure (CPAP) machine to keep airways open.

Insomnia treatments vary. If sleeplessness is due to poor sleep habits, the insomniac should follow the steps for developing better sleep hygiene. Additionally, the sleeper should avoid

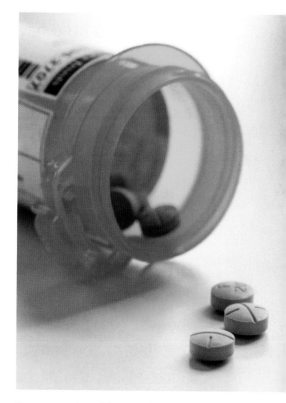

Some people with narcolepsy take Adderall to treat episodes of daytime sleepiness. Other medications can help those with hypersomnia stay awake.

all naps. Often, this is enough to help the insomniac enjoy at least several hours of uninterrupted sleep. If occasional insomnia continues, the sleeper can turn to relaxation techniques at home—imagery, muscle relaxation, or deep breathing. As with any new habit, mastering healthy sleep techniques takes practice. Some insomniacs may need the help of a therapist who specializes in sleep problems to change long-term bad sleeping habits. If all else fails, a doctor may prescribe a sleep medication.

Insomniacs who have certain medical conditions need good sleep habits and more. They require treatment for the emotional or physical problems causing the insomnia. A psychotherapist can treat depression, anxiety, panic attacks, or mood disorders with talk therapy and possibly with medications. Someone with arthritis, back pain, or other conditions that cause insomnia must get treatment for those conditions. Insomniacs who are dependent on alcohol, caffeine, or stimulant drugs must work to end these habits, which affect health in general and sleep patterns in particular.

Narcoleptics need a clear diagnosis from a sleep specialist who will coordinate treatment. Therapy will often begin in a sleep lab to confirm suspected narcolepsy. The doctor will suggest ways the narcoleptic can manage daytime sleep attacks with frequent naps and a flexible work or school schedule. The specialist will probably also suggest regular exercise to promote sleep and good general health. Exercise is also an effective way to manage the stress that can come with narcolepsy. Doctors sometimes prescribe the stimulant Ritalin to narcoleptics, as well as other stimulant drugs. When cataplectic muscle weakness is present, the specialist may prescribe certain antidepressants. Doctors manage narcoleptics' symptoms differently depending on age, lifestyle, and the severity of symptoms.

Restless legs syndrome (RLS) sufferers can take preventive measures to minimize this aggravating disorder. Sufferers should avoid alcohol, caffeine, and cigarettes. Taking baths or massaging the legs can ease some of the crawling sensations in the legs, ankles, or feet before sleep. Someone with RLS who has diabetes or lacks certain vitamins or iron should manage the condition under

Nightmares

Nightmares are bad dreams that can awaken a person from deep REM sleep. They are not the same as sleep terrors, which take place during non-REM stages. Dreamers can remember nightmares but not terrors. Children sometimes experience nightmares, or a series of them, after an upsetting experience. The experience may have happened to them, or it may be something they saw in a movie, on television, or in real life. Being overtired, eating too close to bedtime, drinking alcohol, and taking some medications can all cause nightmares. Talking about upsetting experiences during the day can help a person deal with difficult emotions that contribute to nightmares.

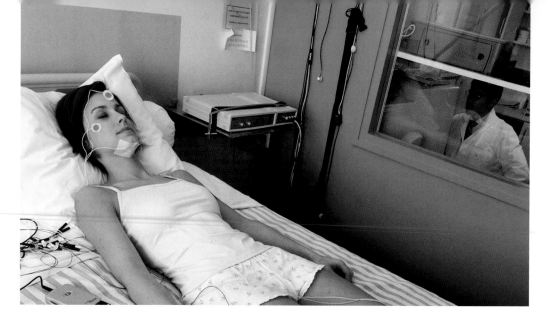

Recording muscle activity during sleep can help a doctor diagnose restless leg syndrome or other movement disorders that interfere with sleep.

medical supervision. New medications can help treat many cases of RLS.

Rhythmic movement disorders such as head banging and body rocking can usually be managed with preventive home treatment. Toddlers or preschoolers usually outgrow this bedtime habit. It is helpful for the child to follow calming routines before bed, such as reading or listening to bedtime stories, singing lullabies, and quietly talking before sleep. The child should have a regular bedtime every night and a regular morning wake time. A padded headboard, body-size pillows, and even a helmet in extreme cases can all be used protect the child's head and body from banging or rocking.

Sleep apnea in adults can be treated in multiple ways. Preventive measures include losing weight, not smoking and not drinking alcohol, and following healthy lifestyle habits, particularly exercising, to build up lung capacity. Continued breathing problems during sleep require medical attention. A doctor may recommend using special devices to keep the airways open. Some fit over the teeth to keep the mouth from moving forward and blocking air passages. Various surgeries can cut out some tissues that block airways, though these painful and expensive procedures are not always effective. Using a CPAP mask and machine, which keeps airways open, is often recommended for adults.

Sleep terrors and sleepwalking in children frighten parents and siblings. Parents can take preventive measures, including making sure the child does not get overtired. The child should not drink caffeinated beverages. Having a regular bedtime and wake-up time is important. So is performing calming activities before sleep. When anyone experiences night terrors or sleep-walking, calmly "talk" the person back to bed. If necessary, keep stairways barricaded and windows and doors locked. Clear the floor of obstacles that could hurt the sleepwalker. Children usually outgrow both of these disorders. Adults who experience them should also develop regular, calm bedtime routines and additionally seek therapy for anxiety, if that is a problem.

Several sleep disorders are permanent conditions. However, nearly all sleep disorders can be managed to some degree. Common-sense habits can bring about refreshing sleep in most people so that it is as predictable as the sun rising and setting every day.

GLOSSARY

biofeedback—A treatment using special equipment to teach people to control bodily processes, such as tension relief and breathing.

bruxism—The grinding of teeth during sleep.

cataplexy—The loss of some muscle control in a narcoleptic.

circadian rhythm—The biological clock, that directs the timing of the body's activities, such as eating, sleeping, and waking.

cortisol—A hormone the body produces when it is under stress.

delayed sleep phase syndrome (DSPS)—The inability to fall asleep until the middle of the night and to awaken until late morning or afternoon.

depression—A psychological condition in which a person feels unhappy and dissatisfied with life.

dyssomnia—A category of sleep disorders characterized by the inability to fall asleep or stay asleep.

homeostasis—The maintenance of a balanced state in the body.

hormones—Chemical substances that the body produces to help it function.

hypersomnia—Excessive sleepiness.

infant and child sleep apnea—A disorder that causes an infant or child to pause temporarily in regular breathing during sleep.

insomnia—A sleep disorder characterized by the inability to fall asleep or to remain asleep as desired.

melatonin—A chemical the body produces to regulate alertness and sleepiness.

narcolepsy—A sleep disorder caused by a problem in the area of the brain that controls sleep and wake patterns; it causes a person to fall asleep at unpredictable times.

nocturnal enuresis—Bed-wetting while sleeping.

parasomnia—A category of sleep disorders characterized by undesirable behaviors that interfere with the stages of sleep.

pineal gland—A part of the brain that releases the sleep chemical melatonin.

polysomnograph—A machine that records sleep patterns and movements during sleep.

rapid eye movement (REM) sleep—The stage of sleep during which dreaming takes place and eyes move quickly under the eyelids.

restless leg syndrome (RLS)—A sleep disorder characterized by burning, crawling sensations that cause a sleeper to move the legs rapidly for relief.

rhythmic movement disorder (RMD)—Head banging or body rocking during sleep.

sleep apnea—A disorder that causes a sleeper to pause breathing multiple times during sleep for ten or more seconds.

sleep hygiene—The practice of healthy sleep habits.

sleep paralysis—The inability to move while dreaming during REM sleep.

sleep terrors—Activities such as screaming and sleepwalking during non-REM sleep.

sleepwalking—Walking that takes place in non-REM sleep, in which the sleeper gets out of bed but is not conscious of doing so.

sudden infant death syndrome (SIDS)—The death of an infant due to the inability to breathe during sleep.

FIND OUT MORE

Organizations

American Sleep Apnea Association
1424 K Street, NW, Suite 302
Washington, DC 20005
(202) 293-3650
www.sleepapnea.org

Narcolepsy Network
79A Main Street
North Kingston, RI 02852
(888) 292-6522
www.narcolepsynetwork.org

National Sudden Infant Death Resource Center
2115 Wisconsin Avenue, NW, Suite 601
Washington, DC 20007
(866) 866-7437
www.sidscenter.org

Books

Culbert, Timothy and Rebecca Kajander. *Be the Boss of Your Sleep: Self-Care for Kids*. Minneapolis, MN: Free Sprit Publishing, 2007.

Epstein, Lawrence and Steven Mardon. *The Harvard Medical School Guide to a Good Night's Sleep*. New York: The McGraw-Hill Companies, 2006.

Foldvary-Schaefer, Nancy. *Getting a Good Night's Sleep: A Cleveland Clinic Guide*. Cleveland, OH: Cleveland Clinic Press, 2006.

Hirshkowitz, Max and Patricia B. Smith. *Sleep Disorders for Dummies*. Indianapolis, IN: Wiley Publishing, Inc., 2004.

Weissbluth, Marc, M.D. *Healthy Sleep Habits, Happy Child*. New York: Ballantine Publishing Group, 2005.

Web Sites

The Better Sleep Council
www.bettersleep.org

Narcolepsy Network
www.narcolepsynetwork.org

Sleepnet.com
www.sleepnet.com

Stanford University Sleep Quest
www.sleepquest.com and www.stanford.edu/~dement/children

INDEX

Page numbers for illustrations are in **boldface**

ABOUT THE AUTHOR

L. H. Colligan writes about many topics, from study skills to activity books and children's fiction. She once worked for a health foundation that promoted prevention as the best way to stay healthy. Her favorite preventive steps for sleeping well are exercising outdoors, eating healthy meals, and reading good books before going to bed. She lives in the Hudson Valley in New York State.